Mrs Carter 6

MACDONALD START

Seashore

Macdonald Educational

About Macdonald Starters

Macdonald Starters are vocabulary controlled information books for young children. More than ninety per cent of the words in the text will be in the reading vocabulary of the vast majority of young readers. Word and sentence length have also been carefully controlled.

Key new words associated with the topic of each book are repeated with picture explanations in the Starters dictionary at the end. The dictionary can also be used as an index for teaching children to look things up.

Teachers and experts have been consulted on the content and accuracy of the books.

Illustrated by: William Robertshaw

Editors: Peter Usborne, Su Swallow Jennifer Vaughan

Reading consultant: Donald Moyle, author of *The Teaching of Reading* and senior lecturer in education at Edge Hill College of Education

Chairman, teacher advisory panel: F. F. Blackwell, general inspector for schools, London Borough of Croydon, with responsibility for primary education

Teacher panel: Elizabeth Wray, Loveday Harmer, Lynda Snowdon, Joy West

Second impression 1972
Made and printed in Great Britain by Purnell & Sons Limited Paulton, nr Bristol

First published 1971 by Macdonald and Company (Publishers) Limited
St Giles House
49-50 Poland Street
London W1

I am on top of a big cliff.
I can see the seashore far below.

Some of the seashore is sandy.
This is called a beach.

Some people swim near the beach.
Some people sail in boats.
One man skis on the water.
A speedboat pulls him along.

Some of the seashore is rocky.
There are rocks under the water.
Once a ship hit the rocks.
Now the old ship is a wreck.

There is a lighthouse on the rocks.
It shines a light at night.
It tells sailors where the rocks are.

There is a sandbank under the water.
Buoys tell sailors
where the sand is.

Ships sail round the sandbank
into the harbour.
Fishermen live round the harbour.

The harbour wall keeps the waves out.
The fishing boats are safe.

A river runs into the harbour.
Boats can go up the river.

This is a big fishing boat.
It has a net.
The net catches lots of fish.

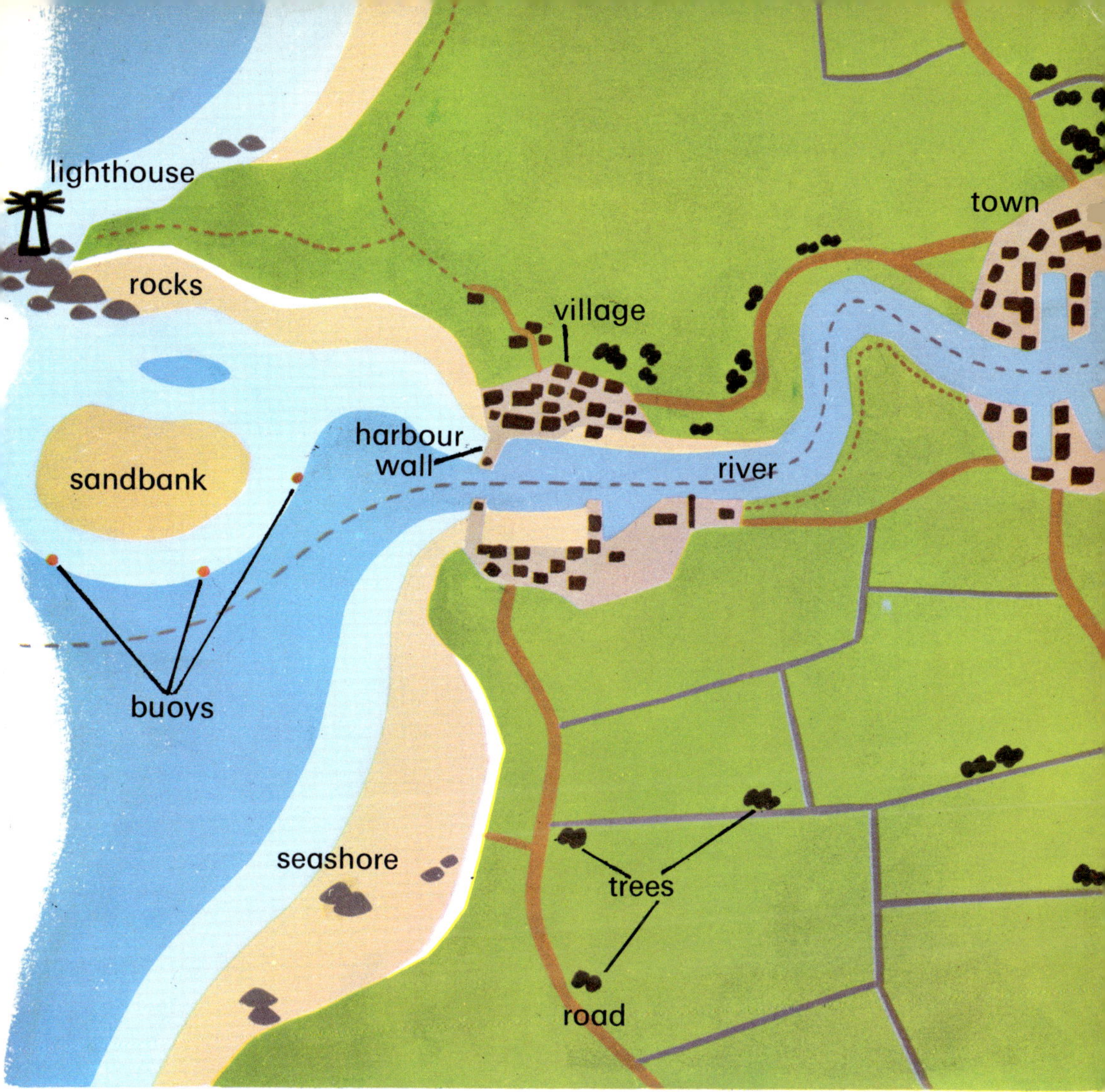

Here is a map.
You can see the land and the sea.
You can see the harbour, the beach,
the rocks and the lighthouse.

It is a high tide.
The waves hit the cliffs.

It is low tide.
The sea has gone down.
Some water stays behind in rock pools.

You can see animals
in some rock pools.

There is seaweed on the rocks.
Some animals with shells
stick to the rocks.

Some animals live in the sand.
This one has a foot for digging.

Worms live in mud sand too.
Some worms squirt sand out.
Some worms look like flowers.

There are pebbles on the seashore.
Pebbles are bits of rock.
The sea makes some pebbles smooth.

Some pebbles are beautiful.
People put them in rings.

There are beaches all over the world.
This beach is in Africa.

This beach is in Australia.
The waves are very high.
Men ride on surfboards.

See for yourself

Look for colours on the seashore.
Collect red things. Collect green things.
Collect other colours too.

Starter's **Seashore** words

cliff
(page 1)

beach
(page 2)

swim
(page 3)

sail
(page 3)

ski
(page 3)

rocks
(page 4)

shipwreck
(page 4)

lighthouse
(page 5)

sailor
(page 5)

sand-bank
(page 6)

buoy
(page 6)

harbour
(page 7)

fisherman
(page 7)

fishing boat
(page 8)

river
(page 9)

net
(page 10)

map
(page 11)

high
tide
(page 12)

waves
(page 12)

low tide
(page 13)

rock
pool
(page 13)

sea-
weed
(page 15)

worm
(page 17)

pebbles
(page 18)